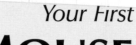

Your First
MOUSE

CONTENTS

Front cover painting by:
D A Lish

Photos by:
**Colin Jeal,
Eric Jukes**

©1999 by Kingdom Books PO9 5TL ENGLAND

INTRODUCTION

To all intents and purposes, a mouse seems to be a very small and insignificant mammal. It is not a voracious hunter and is itself hunted by countless predators, from tawny owls to giant toads, from cats to corn snakes. It is not exactly a plant eater either. No, the mouse is more of a scavenger, picking up what it can, where it can. Yet, for all this, the house mouse, *Mus Musculus*, is one of the most successful animal species on the face of the earth. Why? The answer is simple: from its points of origin in Asia, the mouse, remaining largely unseen, quickly spread out and colonised the world alongside man. Wherever man settled, there the mouse settled.

Every village, town and city in the world has colonies of mice within its dwellings, or underground, or in grain stores, warehouses, and factories. Yes, the mouse is a very successful animal, although often a much maligned one also. Because of their scavenging and gnawing activities, mice have been classified as vermin, as indeed have most members of the order Rodentia, to which they belong.

A Chinchilla explores its environment.

Mice are best kept in single-sexed combinations unless you intend to breed.

But there are other sides to the mouse. There is a particular fascination about it. Countless stories have been written about mice, many of them classics: *Mrs Frisby and the Rats of Nimh*, by Robert O'Brien; *The Tale of Mrs Tittlemouse, The Tale of Two Bad Mice*, and *The Tale of Johnny Town Mouse* by Beatrix Potter; and, pre-dating all of them by some 2000 years, Horace's famous story of the Town Mouse and his cousin the Country Mouse. In entertainment, mice make great cartoon characters. Everyone must have seen the wily Jerry running rings around his hapless foil Tom the cat in the *Tom and Jerry* cartoons. Then there is the most famous celluloid mouse of them all: *Mickey Mouse*, created by Walt Disney in 1928 and still going strong today. But quite apart from all of this, mice make great pets for young and old alike.

Mice have been domesticated for many hundreds of years, the earliest records of such pets coming from the royal palaces of ancient China and Japan. Thanks to the surge of interest in mice and exhibition livestock in the late 19th century, many new colours and varieties were developed. These have enabled domesticated mice, like their wild ancestors, to spread all around the world.

SELECTION

Before buying your first mouse - or indeed any other pet animal - you must first ask yourself a few basic questions:

- Why do you want a mouse? Do you want it purely as a pet or as a show animal?
- Do you want to keep one mouse, or more?
- If you are keeping several mice, what sex will they be?
- If you will be keeping mice of both sexes, presumably you will be breeding them. Can you be sure of finding homes for the offspring?
- If the mouse is for a child, can you be sure that (a) the child wants a mouse, (b) he or she will continue to care for it once the novelty has worn off, and (c) if the child in question is not yours, the parents will give their permission for the child to keep a mouse?

A mouse makes a good pet as it does not take up a great deal of room.

Having considered all of these points (and answered positively in each case!) you are ready to go out and select your pet. For the sake of simplicity, let us assume that you are aiming to keep one mouse. All the information given in this book applies whether you keep one mouse or many.

A Black-eyed Cream shows off its sensitive whiskers.

Buying A Mouse

First of all, where do you go to get your mouse? Do not believe the ridiculous statement found in some books that wild mice, once caught, are easily tamed and make good pets. They do not! Quite apart from the tameness factor, wild mice carry all kinds of unpleasant parasites and often a fair selection of diseases (admittedly through no real fault of their own), so it is pointless even to think of keeping them. Domesticated mice are clean and tame, definitely not to be confused with their wild relatives.

Naturally most people think of the pet shop as a source of mice, and they are right: most pet shops stock mice. Before you make your selection, there are some important factors that must be considered. For instance, are the mice kept in mixed sex colonies? If so, the chances are that you may end up with a pregnant female. If you do not want to breed mice, this could be a big problem. Also, look carefully at the seller's premises. Are they clean, bright, and well organised? Are all the animals housed in clean, spacious accommodation in bright, cheerful surroundings? Can the staff provide the information that you need? Again, ask some questions. Can the staff sex the mice? How old are the mice? What is their preferred diet? Do the staff seem nervous about handling the mice, or do the mice themselves seem nervous? If these questions can be answered in a positive manner, then you can proceed.

If your pet shop does not have the particular colour variety that you want, perhaps the dealer can order it for you. If not, maybe you can contact a local mouse breeder. Of course, this is not as easy as it sounds, because very few mouse breeders are listed in the telephone directory. A mouse club is a possible point of contact. Details of such clubs can be obtained from registers of clubs and societies, which are available in your local library. Alternatively, you can write to the author care of TFH Publications, PO Box 74, Havant PO9 5TL, England. Please remember to enclose a stamped, self-addressed envelope or International Reply Coupon as appropriate.

Once you have made contact with a breeder, visit his house, and look at it in the same way that you did the pet shop. It is just as important that the conditions are clean and bright. Remember to ask the relevant questions about your mouse: its age, sex, hereditary background, preferred housing, best food, and so on. Remember also to bring a strong box or another type of suitable container in which to transport your mouse: breeders do not always keep a supply of such containers, nor should you expect them to.

What To Look For

The average mouse should measure some 10cm in length, excluding the tail, which should be as long as the body. Of course, there are many different varieties from which to choose, but the general 'type' in each mouse is the same. The coat should be even and clean, with no bald patches. Whether the coat is long or short, it should be smooth and glossy. Satinized mice have extra glossy coats, but the general rule applies. Curly-coated mice often have natural 'baldness' when young, so make allowances for this: be guided by what you learn from the person who is selling you the mouse.

Check that there are neither parasites in the fur, nor that the skin is flaky. The mouse's ears should be large and erect - in fact, almost tulip-shaped, as specified in the mouse judging standards. The eyes should be bold, bright and clear, and free from any dullness or discharge. The nose should be clean and twitching, the whiskers long and full. The tail should be clean and free of scabs or bites. Also, run your index finger and thumb along the mouse's tail, checking for kinks. If you intend to use the mouse for breeding, a badly kinked tail will lead to a genetical fault in the offspring: they too will have kinked tails. A show mouse will be disqualified because of this fault. Look at each foot in turn, checking carefully that all of the toes are intact. The mouse should be pleasantly sleek: neither thin or wasted nor overweight. An obese mouse will not have good health prospects. If a female mouse (doe) is extra large over the flanks, then the chances are that she is pregnant, so avoid buying her, unless you want lots of baby mice. Finally, observe how the mouse behaves. It should be alert and reasonably active. It should not be skittish or nervous. If a mouse bites when approached, have nothing to do with it as a pet.

One very important factor to bear in mind is smell. Despite what some books say, mice do smell. Males (bucks) have a particularly strong odour, and this must be borne in mind when you select either a single mouse or a single-sex pair. Does have a slight smell, but it is not nearly as noticeable as in bucks. If you do want a single-sex pair of mice, then two does will do nicely. Not only would two bucks smell more strongly, but the chances are that they would fight for supremacy as well.

As previously mentioned, mice are not really cuddly or loving pets, so do not expect to see your mouse run up to its handler, lick him and try to snuggle up to him. A good mouse is one that will sit calmly but remain alert, or climb around on its handler without any sign of fright or panic. This is the mouse for you!

When selecting your pet mouse look for an even and clean coat, with no bald patches.

This Lilac Self is one of the new colours developed in recent years.

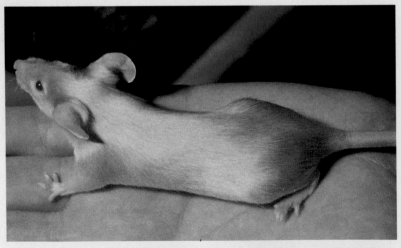

The coat of the Argente Satin has a high sheen, described in the standard as 'an exquisite satin-like or metallic gloss'.

Hold the tail to prevent the mouse from leaping off your hand.

A Black Self.

HOUSING

Being relatively small animals, mice do not need tremendously large or complicated housing. Most pet shops stock a wide variety of cages, many specifically designed for mice, that are perfectly suitable.

What Type Of Cage?

One of the most popular mouse cages is the kind with a sturdy plastic or metal base and a wire canopy over the top. This type of cage is not only attractive but also easy to clean and enables you to see your mouse. The minimum cage size for one mouse or a pair of mice is 30cm x 20cm x 20cm. As mice are past masters at squeezing through small spaces, the bar gauge (the space between the bars) should be no more than 8mm. Often, this type of cage is sold as a hamster cage, in which case the bar gauge is somewhat wider, so make sure that you get the correct gauge.

Another suitable type of cage is made of either metal or thick wood, with solid sides and a sliding glass front. Sometimes the glass front extends up to two-thirds of the cage's height, the remainder of the area being metal bars. Again, the minimum dimensions apply. This type of cage often has a nest box fitted on the inside, with a ladder running up to it. This is ideal, as mice like to climb and enjoy a secure nest area. However, experience shows that a nest box without a lid or roof is preferable, as nest boxes often overheat when packed with bedding and mice.

Aquarium tanks, constructed of either plastic or glass, make excellent cages for mice. The advantage of an aquarium tank is that it affords all-around vision while keeping the occupants warm and snug, safe from draughts. Conversely, of course, it is necessary to ensure that the tank is not placed in direct sunlight or a hot area, as the greenhouse effect takes on a whole new meaning and the occupants will suffer. An aquarium tank will need a lid. Often such tanks come with a lid, but it is best to discard it, as what may be suitable for fish is not suitable for mice. A lid intended for an aquarium does not allow for the necessary ventilation. Instead, you will need to construct a lid out of small-gauge wire: the more solid, the better. Chicken wire breaks up too easily and often a persistent mouse can actually gnaw through it or make the holes in the chicken wire bigger and thus escape.

Mice are nothing if not persistent... so whatever type of cage you choose, beware of the activities of the 'escape committee'!

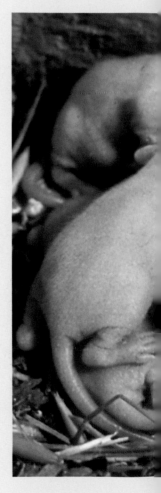

Basic Cage Requirements

To start with, you need substrate - a covering for the floor. Sawdust is by far the best substrate for mice. Wood shavings are also acceptable, but experience shows that mice prefer a finer, softer floor cover. It is always best to purchase sawdust direct from a pet shop, where it will (or should!) be packaged in pre-medicated bags. Of course, you can buy sawdust direct from a lumberyard, but remember that then you are running the risk of contamination by preservation or of foreign bodies in the sawdust.

Baby mice are born naked, blind and deaf.

Mice like to make nests, so bedding is definitely required. Ignore what you may have read about shredded newspaper being acceptable; it is not. Printed paper can be toxic to small animals. Once again, your pet shop should be able to meet your requirements for bedding. Avoid fibre-based bedding, especially the kind with a nylon base. The fibres are hard and sharp and can cause horrific injuries to small animals, such as severing toes or feet. Soft shredded paper makes ideal bedding and is not expensive. This kind of paper, of course, is not printed and is often pre-medicated. The very best bedding is hay. Not only is it warm, but also the mice can eat it and it provides good roughage in their diet.

A food bowl is another necessary item. Preferably a solid earthenware or metal one that cannot be tipped over easily. Plastic bowls are tippable and, not surprisingly, get chewed up very quickly. Water is best provided by means of a gravity water bottle as opposed to a bowl, which can get filled with sawdust and soak up all the water, not to mention making a mess. Bottles are provided with special hangers for most cages. If your mouse is housed in an aquarium tank, it is a fairly simple matter to make a 'cradle hanger' out of wire, in which the bottle can be suspended from the wire-mesh lid or hooked over the side of the tank.

Furnishings

Many commercially-made cages come complete with certain basic furnishings such as nest boxes. If your cage does not have any such furnishings, then it is up to you to provide them. Often nest boxes can be bought separately. Small bird nest boxes can be used. Plastic hamster houses may also be used but may be gnawed. Again, be mindful of the fact that the box is best without a lid. Alternatively, you can just leave it to the mice by providing them with plenty of bedding material. They will choose where to make a nest, usually in the corner of the cage.

Mice do not really go in for toys as such. They are not ultra-intelligent animals and do not need to be stimulated through play. However, cardboard tubes from toilet tissue and paper towel rolls are often used as makeshift burrows and are also relished for gnawing activities. Regarding the matter of gnawing: mice, being rodents, do need to exercise their chisel-like incisor teeth. To a certain extent, the basic good dry diet should take care of this, but if you want to make doubly sure that this need is met, place a small block of wood in the cage for this purpose. If the mice do express a desire to gnaw (and not all mice do) then this will prevent them from damaging parts of their cage.

Mice are quite acrobatic, and you will get used to the sight of one walking upside down underneath the cage lid or climbing the bars. A couple of ladders will always be appreciated. They can be bought from a pet shop, where they are sold for birds such as budgies and cockatiels. With the gnawing factor in mind, it is best to avoid plastic ladders and choose metal ones instead. You do not have to buy a proper ladder, as a branch or thick twig does just as well. Make sure that you wash branches and twigs before giving them to the mice. In time, they will probably get gnawed away, but the beauty of this is that they can be replaced easily.

Swings are also welcome and can be hung from the top of the cage or lid. Again, bird accessories such as metal swings are ideal.

Exercise Wheel

Many cages come complete with exercise wheels, which are useful, as many mice enjoy taking a spin on them. Some wheels are pathetically small, even for mice. The best rule of thumb is 'the bigger, the better', so a wheel that allows a mouse to trundle around without being cramped or hunched is perfect. It is best to use a solid wheel as opposed to the spoke variety, as nasty accidents can occur when the tail gets trapped.

Cage Location

Situate the cage in an area protected from draughts, direct sunlight, or excessive heat. The optimum room temperature range for mice is between 15-19°C. Make sure the cage cannot be knocked down or the occupants bothered by young children or household pets.

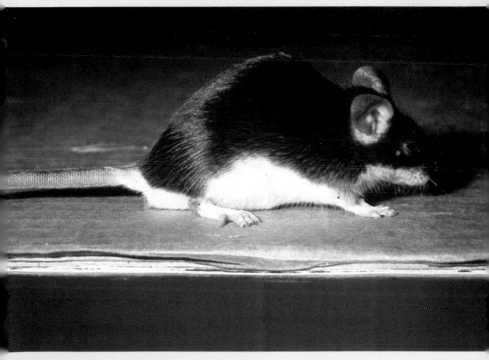

Be sure to allow your mouse supervised time away from his cage.

FEEDING

When considering the correct diet for your mouse, forget all the old wives' tales and cartoon baloney about mice living on cheese. Most mice, even wild ones, do not like cheese anyway, as it is often far too strong in flavour and smell for their palates. Like any other pet animal, your mouse requires a well-balanced diet that is suitable for its needs. What it eats might not seem attractive or interesting to you, but it is what is good for the mouse that is important.

Your pet needs a good, balanced diet in order to keep in prime condition.

Basic Diet

The bulk of the mouse's diet consists of dry food. The best combination of this is clipped or rolled oats, mixed corn, flaked maize, and dried, crushed peas. Usually, you can obtain a good basic dry food mixture from your pet shop. It may be either in the form of a proprietary brand or something that the shop mixes itself. With the prepared brands, you must check the contents carefully. A dry mix can contain a large proportion of rabbit pellets, sunflower seeds and peanuts. Often mice totally reject the rabbit pellets on the grounds of taste. Sunflower seeds and peanuts will, however, be readily eaten but they can cause problems as both are very rich in protein. A mouse can react to too much protein, leading to sores and spots on the skin and loss of condition. A few of these items in the mix are all well and good; but if they are the dominant constituents, you are asking for trouble. To ensure that your mouse receives the correctly balanced dry food, it may be advisable to buy the different constituents and make up a mix yourself. Alternatively, the pet shop may make you up a mix on bulk order.

Sometimes, a proprietary mix contains dog biscuits. This is good, as dog biscuits are useful in giving the mice something extra to gnaw and are also quite nutritious. If the mix does not contain them, you can always buy a few to add or just leave them in the cage for the mice to gnaw when the mood strikes them. Always remember to remove them after a couple of days, in case they go mouldy.

Small amounts of dog biscuits, sunflower seeds and peanuts can all be added to the basic grain mix above.

Stale bread is also a good, integral part of the diet. Do not worry about the fact that the bread is stale; this makes it harder, which the mice prefer. Be sensible about the degree of staleness; the bread should be no more than five days old otherwise mould will probably develop.

Greens

As a supplement to the basic diet, you can give your pets some greens, in the form of fruit or vegetables. Quite apart from the vitamins that such foodstuffs contain, they also contain a good degree of moisture. Avoid the different types of lettuce, as they have very little nutritional value and can be a major cause of diarrhoea.

Root crops such as carrot, turnip, and swede are good and filling. Cabbage and sprouts are acceptable, as are peas, spinach, watercress and cauliflower leaves.

More 'natural' greens can include chickweed, dandelion and fresh young grass shoots. If you are picking any kind of vegetable from your own garden, make sure

A Champion Argente show mouse.

that you wash it thoroughly before feeding to your mice. In fact, washing all greens is basic hygiene, especially as many commercially-produced items are sprayed with pesticides. On the fruit front, the best fruit by far is apple, with tomato as second best. Citrus fruits should be avoided as they contain a high level of citric acid which can be harmful to small animals' stomachs. Any greens should be given sparingly and then only as a supplement to the basic diet. In addition, they should not be given too frequently: once or twice a week is quite enough.

Drinking Water
Although greens contain a high level of moisture, always ensure that your mouse has clean fresh water every day. Mice drink a lot, especially in warm weather, as they can dehydrate very quickly.

Supplements
Occasionally, a bowl of bread and milk provides a welcome change, being a good source of vitamin B and calcium. Bread can also be soaked in water and placed in a bowl as an additional source of moisture when required - perhaps during hot weather or when you are away for a day or two - thus ensuring that the mice have adequate food and moisture at all times. Pregnant or nursing mice appreciate some bread and milk, which helps the mother build up her energy reserves. Also, young mice will develop quickly with access to this supplement.

Provided that your mouse receives a well-balanced diet, additional vitamins and minerals are not necessary.

Mice cannot see very well, but use their large ears to pick up information about their surroundings.

HANDLING

When you first bring your mouse home, put it in its cage with a supply of food and water and then leave it alone for a few hours. This allows the mouse to explore its new home and get acquainted with the layout of things. Mice are territorial creatures, especially bucks, and they often mark their territory in the same way as other animals, by urinating or defecating in strategic areas. Generally, however, your mouse will reserve a particular area of the cage for its toilet. As mentioned earlier, bucks' urine does have a rather pungent odour, but this is much less noticeable with females.

Taming And Training

The first stage in taming your pet is getting it used to a regular routine and, more importantly, to you. Mice have an excellent sense of smell and soon identify their owners in this way. Also, your body language plays a great part in putting the mouse at ease. Inexperienced people often make sharp, nervous movements that unsettle their pets. So, be slow and gentle in your movements near the cage. Talk to the mouse, not just when you are feeding it, but whenever you are near it. Although the mouse will not understand a word that you are saying, it will associate your voice with you. In this way, the mouse can build up a picture of you via smell, movement, and sound. Its eyesight is not good so it won't recognise you visually, other than by your body movements.

After two or three days, your mouse should be sufficiently calm and sure of you for you to attempt the next stage of the procedure. The way to any animal's heart is through its stomach, so put a tasty titbit of food between your finger and thumb and then offer it to the mouse through the bars of the cage, or from above. The mouse will probably sniff at you and the food and then, if it feels safe enough, it will take the titbit in its mouth and scurry off to eat it. Try this method three or four times until the mouse is fully at ease. It might even run up to the cage bars or stand on its hind legs when it sees you approach. Now put your hand into the cage, with the titbit on your palm. Don't move, especially not suddenly - let the mouse come to you. With a bit of luck, it will hop onto your hand and take the titbit. Hopefully, it will become sufficiently brave to eat the titbit while sitting on your palm. Remember to talk to it quietly all the time to reassure it. Try this again two or three times to gain the mouse's confidence.

When you attempt this next and the mouse sits on your palm, gently close your fingers around the mouse's midriff and lift it up. If it panics, it may nip you. Accept this - and then put it down again. Once more, try putting your fingers around it until you can lift it out of the cage. You can hold the tail close to its base to keep the mouse from jumping off your palm. By now, the mouse should be very confident, so let it run along your arm. It is a good idea at this stage to sit on a chair or a sofa and let the mouse run over you. Let it wander off onto the chair or sofa but be ready to grab it if it decides to make a break for freedom. Stroke the mouse gently and keep talking to it. In a short space of time, the mouse should be tame and confident in your company.

For speed and convenience, mice may also be picked up by their tails but only do this to transfer them to your palm or to the cage. Always remember to grasp the tail close to its base, or root. If you hold the mouse by the tip of its tail, this will hurt the mouse and you may incur its wrath. Also, the skin may come off the tail, which is very painful for the mouse.

Some people like to train their pets. Of the rodents, rats are the most intelligent and thus the easiest to train, performing all kinds of entertaining tricks. On a more scientific note, rats are often used in laboratory experiments to study behaviour and learning. Mice, although capable of learning elementary routines, are not the most intelligent of rodents and so cannot learn to perform such complex tasks. However, if you really want to try teaching your mouse some tricks and you are prepared to put in several hours' effort, then why not?

Remember to keep the edible treat factor in the mouse's mind, and you may manage to teach it to climb up ropes or ladders to obtain a reward. It might also be fun for you to construct a mini-maze out of cardboard or plastic tubes and cardboard strips. You can create walls and corridors, down which the mouse has to run to find its reward. As long as you do not expect too much, training your pet mouse can be an interesting experience.

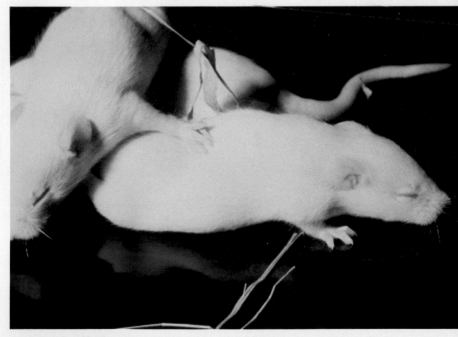

Nine-day-old Baby Creams. The fur has grown, but the eyes have not yet opened.

BREEDING

Mice are among the most prolific of all animals. They have a high fertility rate, a short gestation period, and they reach maturity very quickly. Without trotting out that old chestnut about how many offspring may descend from an original pair of mice, suffice to say that uncontrolled breeding can be a grave error. Quite apart from any other consideration, it is not fair to the mice.

Before you start on the process of breeding your mice (and we shall assume for this chapter that you have at least one sexed pair of mice) you must consider a few questions similar to those asked when you decided to keep mice in the first place:

- Do you have enough cages for a breeding project? You will need one for each buck and doe in a pair, possibly more if you have other does. You will also need at least one other cage to house the offspring when they are weaned.
- Do you have the means of finding homes for the surplus offspring? You certainly will not want to keep them all.
- If you intend to sell excess mice, are you hoping to make an income from it? If so, forget it, unless you own a mouse farm with hundreds of customers queuing up to buy your mice to the point of placing advance orders. Nobody ever made a fortune from mice! (Except, perhaps, Walt Disney...)
- And especially for the younger reader: make sure you obtain your parents' permission before you embark on this course of action.

The Mating Process

Mice reach sexual maturity between 6 and 12 weeks of age, but it is best not to breed them too young. The usual breeding formula is to run a buck with two or more does. It is not simply a matter of leaving them all together to allow nature to take its course; breeding mice is a far more precise science than that. To begin with, breeding adults should be selected with a number of important factors in mind: size, stamina, and type (the actual shape and composition of the mouse by which all mice are initially judged), to say nothing of careful selection for the required variety. This kind of knowledge comes with experience, so do not expect to know it all from the word go. If you are interested in exhibiting fancy mice and want to breed some good specimens, ask some more experienced fanciers.

Ovulation in mice lasts between four and six days, with the heat lasting for up to 12 hours. At this time, the doe is at the peak of fertility, and the buck will quickly mate her.

The Dutch is a difficult variety to breed. In this example, there is a good blaze between the eyes, but the saddle does not start far enough up the back.

Pregnancy is soon very noticeable, with the doe's body swelling greatly, especially over the flanks. At this point, the doe is said to be 'in kindle' and may now be removed to her own cage to have her litter, or 'to kindle'. Unless you want wall-to-wall mice, do not leave the removal of the doe or buck until after the litter is born. Mice are subject to a condition known as postpartum oestrus: that is, the doe goes into heat immediately after the litter is born, whereupon the buck will immediately mate her again.

It is a fallacy to say that buck mice will eat a newborn litter. In fact, many make good fathers, nestling down with the babies while the doe takes a breather. However, it is always best to separate the prospective parents before the litter is born. This prevents the undue strain on the doe if she becomes pregnant while rearing the first litter. Her bodily resources will be divided between both litters, born and unborn, with the result that neither litter will enjoy optimum development.

Gestation

Mice have a short gestation period, lasting between 18 and 21 days. During the last few days of pregnancy, you must provide the doe with extra bedding and increase her amount of food, perhaps adding some extra wheatgerm, together with bread and milk. Two or three pregnant does can litter together in the same cage, as long as the babies will be born within a couple of days of each other, so that they are all at roughly the same stage of development. Two or more does will often make a communal nest and suckle all the babies together. Obviously this method is to be avoided if you want to be sure which babies belong to a particular doe, in which case she should be housed on her own.

The Litter

Usually the doe will give birth to her litter in the evening or early hours of the morning. Each baby is delivered in an individual birth sac, which the doe bites off and eats. She then cleans up the baby and adds it to the nest. The babies are born naked, blind and deaf, able only to suckle from their mother. The average litter size is between eight and ten, although litters of up to 18 are not unknown! It is best not to disturb the nest for a day or two, even if the doe is a placid and trusting mouse. Instances of does eating their offspring are fairly rare but, if a nursing mother panics, she may do just that to protect her litter. Also, the doe may well dispose of any dead or sickly offspring herself, getting the litter to a manageable size.

The babies grow quickly; after a few days, their ears open and they squeak more frequently, perhaps to communicate with each other. The fur begins to grow at around four days, and markings on any marked or patterned varieties should also become apparent at this time. The babies' eyes open at 14 days, and they begin to scurry around. Often, the poor doe gets quite harassed and has to carry her babies back into the nest, rather like a female cat does with her kittens. The babies begin to nibble at solid food at around ten days of age and quickly learn to seek out food, although they will continue to suckle for about another ten days. At this point, remember to provide extra food for the babies. A bread-and-milk mixture is an ideal supplement to give them added calcium and vitamin B, thus promoting their growth and development. The litter should be weaned between 21 and 28 days of age and removed to their own cage.

After this, you will have to sex them. Sexing mice is easy; the best method is to hold the mouse up by the tail and inspect the groin area. The distance between the urethra and anus is greater in bucks than in does. Does also have two rows of nipples, which are often quite visible, down their abdomen. Remember that mice reach sexual maturity very quickly, so the bucks and does must be split up into single-sex groups by no later than six weeks of age. Mice are considered to be fully adult at eight weeks of age, which is in keeping with their relatively short lifespan.

The doe, having raised her litter, can be returned to her friends, but must be rested for a couple of weeks to allow her to get back into condition before she is mated again. Carefully used, a good doe can produce up to ten litters in her lifetime. Bucks can often remain virile until the day they die, but generally speaking, virility fades after 12 to 14 months.

The lack of fur on these baby mice indicates that they are only a few days old.

VARIETIES

There are over 40 different varieties of domesticated, or fancy, mice which have been developed over the past 100 years. Some of the varieties are extremely rare nowadays, and some are still being developed. The different varieties of mice are grouped together under different 'type' classifications: Self (one colour); Tan (with a tan-coloured belly); Marked (Patterned Varieties); Any Other Variety (AOV) (varieties not covered by the other classifications); and Coat Varieties (mice with different fur types). Each variety conforms to its own Standard of Excellence. In the United kingdom, these Standards are laid down by the National Mouse Club (NMC), the governing body of the mouse fancy in this country. In America, one of the largest organisations for mouse fanciers is the American Fancy Rat and Mouse Association. In a book this size, it would be impossible to list every individual variety and its full standard. What follows is a basic description of the varieties that you are most likely to find in a pet shop.

Selfs
Selfs are mice with one overall body colour and no other markings. The eye colour varies in different breeds, depending on certain genetical traits relating to that colour. For instance, you may well find white mice with either pink or black eyes. The pink-eyed specimens are true albinos (animals with no colouration whatsoever) while black-eyed specimens are not true albinos. This can get a little confusing, as what looks like a black-eyed white mouse may, in fact, be classed as a Cream, an 'off-white' mouse with black eyes. Other popular Selfs include Black, Chocolate, Dove (a soft grey), Red Fawn (a pale orange), Champagne (the colour of 'champagne silk', as in the Mouse Standards) and Blue (a medium slate-blue).

Tans
The Tan group consists of mice with a recognised top colour and a tan belly. In good specimens the top colour and the tan colour must be clearly separated by a straight demarcation line. Tans are extremely attractive mice, often found for sale.

Marked
Several varieties are covered by this group, although some, such as the Even-Marked and Rump White, are rare. Breeding Marked Mice to a correct standard in which the markings must conform as closely as possible is, as you can imagine, quite a difficult task. There are very few mice in a litter that do conform to the standard. The most commonly found Marked varieties are:

Broken Marked: white, with seven or eight large spots of colour on its body.

Dutch: a very attractive specimen with a patch covering each side of the face, separated by a white blaze. The neck and shoulders are white, joined by a coloured saddle extending to the rump and down half of the tail and back legs. This is an exacting standard, with lots of mis-marked results, but which can be very appealing to the pet mouse owner.

Variegated: white, with patches of colour splashed evenly over its body.

Banded: coloured, with a white band around its midriff.

Any Other Colour

Many different varieties are listed under this grouping. Some are quite exotic; many are rare. Quite a few of them are likely to be found in pet shops.

Seal Point Siamese: rather like the original Siamese cat, the body is coloured medium beige, shading gradually down to a dark point at the tail root. Darker seal points are also to be found on the muzzle, ears and feet.

Agouti: often said to resemble the wild mouse but in reality a lot more attractive than that, with rich brown and golden fur, ticked with black.

Cinnamon: related colour to Agouti, but more of a rust-golden tan, ticked with brown.

Chinchilla: named after the chinchilla itself, or rather the original form of this animal, it is mid-grey, with a slate-blue undercoat and an intermediate shade of pearl grey, with each hair evenly tipped with black.

Coat Varieties

The different coat variations in mice are extremely interesting and attractive. These mice may be any standard recognised colour variety but have different fur types, by which they are primarily judged. They are as follows:

Satin: a relatively recently developed variety. The standard was granted to Mr and Mrs A G Cooke in 1975. Satins have a coat with a high sheen, resulting in 'an exquisite satin-like or metallic gloss', as stated in the NMC Standard. They really are quite sensational and make highly attractive pets as well as exhibition animals.

Astrex: the oldest known 'coat variety', developed by Mr A Tuck. The standard was granted to him in 1936. The coat is extremely curly, often wavy, and the whiskers also curl. Youngsters often start off with tightly curled fur, but it straightens out with various moults by the time they are adult. It is still possible to discern that they are Astrex, but they are often a pale imitation of younger animals. Occasionally, a particular specimen, usually a buck, retains good curling into adulthood. Needless to say, these are the ones to breed.

Long-haired: the second oldest variety in this category, the standard having been granted to Mr A D Jones in 1969. As the name suggests, this variety has long fur, as long and as dense as possible, being of silky texture. As in hamsters, Long-haired bucks have noticeably longer coats than do does.

Rex: this curly-coated variety is not to be confused with the Astrex. Its curls are much closer and denser, almost fuzzy. Young Rex mice have a rather disconcerting appearance, looking almost bald for a number of weeks before their fur moults into its final adult form. Even then, the animal's skin can be seen clearly through the close curls of the coat. Despite this, however, the Rex is a fascinating, if neglected, variety and is currently enjoying a revival of interest among some fanciers. The provisional standard was originally granted to Mrs E Branston in 1975 but lapsed due to lack of fanciers' interest in developing the variety. Currently, the variety has been taken up and developed by Mr Nick Baxter but it remains unstandardised.

The different Coat Varieties make highly attractive pets, especially as they can also be bred in combination with one another, such as Satin Long-haired, Satin Astrex or even Long-haired with Satin Astrex.

Rare Varieties

Several of the more specialised varieties of mouse are quite rare. These mice really are the province of more experienced fanciers but there is always a possibility that some may become available from a breeder as sub-show standard but perfectly acceptable pet-quality animals. Look out for varieties such as Dove, Pearl, Rump White, Tricolour, Blue Point Siamese, and the latest mutation, the Brindle. The Brindle deserves a special mention: appearing almost marbled, the Standard calls for it to 'have streaks, bars, and little ears of any colour over a diluted background'. Unfortunately, this is one of those varieties with a rare 'lethal' genetical factor: only Brindle does survive into adulthood and may be bred. Any bucks usually die within two weeks of birth. This obviously presents a problem as far as correct breeding is concerned. Breeders use a standard coloured buck to mate with a Brindle doe to create a mixture of Brindle and 'normal' coloured offspring. The provisional standard was granted to Steve Haswell in 1990.

Mice are inquisitive creatures but have poor eyesight.

The Mouse Fancy's Beginnings

The first fancy mice were shown in England in 1892 at a show in Oxford. The fact that mouse classes were staged at this show was widely reported in the fanciers' newspaper *Fur & Feather*. This led to several interested mouse breeders getting together and exhibiting mice at a few more shows. By 1895, their numbers had swelled sufficiently to enable them to form a proper mouse club to cater for their needs. Thus it was in December 1895 that the British Mouse Club was founded. The club's name changed the following year to the National Mouse Club (NMC) by which name it is known to this day.

Exhibiting Mice

If you decide that you want to take your interest in fancy mice further than merely keeping them as pets and breeding them, your best approach is to join the mouse fancy and exhibit mice at shows.

The prospective mouse fancier should read about shows in more specialised publications and make direct contact with a local mouse club. This gives you a unique chance to meet other folk with the same interest as yourself. Shows provide a great social forum for people from all walks of life to meet, talk and show mice. Experienced mouse fanciers will nearly always be ready and willing to impart advice and practical help. However, do remember one thing: if you ask for advice, be prepared to listen to more experienced fanciers and act on what you are told. Above all, once you start showing mice and actively participating in the club's affairs, you will gain a great sense of enjoyment and fun, which is born out of good sportsmanship and friendly competition. Best of luck!

A well-handled mouse will be easier to judge than a semi-tame one.

HEALTH

A complete list of possible ailments and their treatment would be impossible in a book this size. What follows is a brief list of the major ailments of mice, with notes about their possible treatment.

Wounds: Mice usually co-exist quite happily in correctly structured groups. Sometimes, however, for whatever reason, fights can occur, more often than not between two bucks. They seldom lead to death but can lead to wounds that need treatment. An untreated wound may get dirty, resulting in an abscess or even a blood infection. To treat, remove the mouse from its cage and gently bathe its wounds in warm water. If the wound looks particularly dirty, a very small amount of diluted antiseptic may be added to the water. If the wound has developed into an abscess, it will need to be opened and emptied. This is done by gently squeezing any pus out into a tissue. Be careful not to squeeze too hard and hurt the mouse which may go into shock. Then bathe the abscess. A drop of hydrogen peroxide will ensure that all pus is cleared out of the abscess. Apply it to the abscess cavity, where it will bubble up upon contact with the flesh, forcing out all the pus.

Mites: These small fur-dwelling parasites can be brought in with untreated hay or sawdust, as well as by infected mice. Treatment is twofold. First dip your mouse in a parasiticide, which may be obtained from a pet shop or a vet. One dip should be enough to eliminate most of the mites. Next, a special 'fly block', or pest strip, which will kill any remaining mites in the area, should be placed in the same room as the mouse's cage. Again, prevention is better than cure, so always have such a device set up if possible.

Diarrhoea: The symptoms are both obvious and smelly. This points to too much green or liquid food being given to your mouse. Simply cut out all vegetables, fruit and wet food for a few days and give only plain dry mix, with fresh drinking water always available. The condition should soon right itself. After a week or so, start feeding the greens again, but in smaller quantities than before. If the condition persists it may be due to a bacterial infection in which case, consult your vet.

Colds: The symptoms of a cold in mice are the same as in humans: runny nose, sneezing, hunched-up appearance, lethargy, and sore eyes. Isolate a mouse with a cold in its own cage in a warmer environment, with extra bedding. Feed it some nutritious supplement, such as bread and milk with cod-liver oil and extra vitamins added. The cold should soon disappear, and, after a week or so, the mouse can be returned to a communal cage.

Waltzing: The mouse turns round and round in circles, losing its balance and acting in a disoriented fashion. It is more commonly known as an affliction of the inner ear. A course of antibiotics from a vet will sometimes arrest the condition, but the cause is usually an incurable hereditary defect. By far the kindest course of action is to have any afflicted mice put to sleep, and no offspring should be used for breeding.

Tumours: These are swellings that develop in the bodies of mice. They can be confused with abscesses, but tumours are usually solid to the touch. Tumours usually develop in the milk glands in does or in the testicles in bucks. There is no cure: eventually these cancerous growths will kill the mouse. It is kindest to put the afflicted individual down before the tumour grows too large. If a particular strain of mice seems prone to tumours, it is best to discontinue breeding from it.

Nest boxes are best left open to prevent their inhabitants from over-heating.

If you would like to take your interest in mice further, you can obtain more information, including details of standards and shows, from The National Mouse Club.

TFH Publications offers the most comprehensive selection of books dealing with mice. A selection of significant titles is presented below; they and many other works are available from your local pet shop.

The National Mouse Club
c/o TFH Publications
PO Box 74
Havant
Hants. PO9 5TT

Tel: 01705 481133

TFH Publications will be able to tell you the address of the current Secretary.

The following publication may also be of interest to you:

Fur and Feather
Elder House
Chattisham
Ipswich
Suffolk. IP8 3EQ

The Guide To Owning A Mouse
Howard Hirschhorn
TFH RE-506
ISBN 0-7938-2155-X
Soft cover: 170mm x 250mm, 64 pages, 58 full colour photos.

Mice as a Hobby
Jack Young
TFH TT-019
ISBN 0-86622-949-3
Soft cover: 170mm x 250mm, 96 pages, 117 full colour photos.

Mice as a New Pet
Richard Pfarr
TFH TU-022
ISBN 0-86622-530
Soft cover: 170mm x 200mm, 64 pages, 77 full colour photos.